DATING
IS ABOUT
FINDING SOMEONE
SO YOU
NEVER
HAVE TO DATE AGAIN

D1124275

DATING
IS ABOUT
FINDING SOMEONE
SO YOU
NEVER
HAVE TO DATE AGAIN

BY

NANCY DAVIDOFF KELTON

ILLUSTRATED BY KEITH BENDIS

Andrews and McMeel

A Universal Press Syndicate Company

Kansas City

Library of Congress Cataloging-in-Publication Data

Kelton, Nancy Davidoff.
    Dating is about finding someone so you never have to date again / by Nancy Davidoff Kelton ; illustrated by Keith Bendis.
        p.   cm.
    ISBN 0-8362-7026-6
    1. Dating (Social customs)—Humor.   I. Title.
PN6231.D3K45   1995
818'.5402—dc20   94–34680
                                         CIP

Articles entitled "The Culture Gap," "Risky Invitations," "87 Things That Are Better Than Sex," and "Is He Dating Material?" have appeared in *New Woman* magazine and articles entitled "Dating at 40" and "You Can't Get Pastrami at the Drugstore" have appeared in *Parents* magazine.

Designed by Barrie Maguire

CONTENTS

CONTENTS

DEDICATION

*For my parents, Max and Esther Davidoff,
and my daughter Emily*

INTRODUCTION

A few words about me. And about the book. So you don't get the wrong idea.

I am a professional writer, not a professional single. I didn't major in dating. I began dating when my marriage ended. It's that simple. That complex. And that nauseating.

Last year, a friend gave my phone number to a man whom she claimed would be "It." He never called.

"He won't be available after all," she told me.

"Why? What did you say about me?"

"Nothing. He died."

"Where's he buried?" I asked.

"A cemetery in Queens."

"You're right," I said. "It's too far away."

Maybe not. I've dated men with addictions, ambivalence, wives they have not *quite* divorced, and a scarcity of testosterone. I've dated men whose libidos are in rest homes. Why is "not breathing" somewhere out in Queens any more unavailable?

A big fear of the *live* men I've encountered is that they will show up in my work. A bigger fear is that they won't. I understand. It's tricky business dating a writer who is writing a book on dating.

Especially if you're a creep.

There was the sixties man who, in 1994, spent the entire evening saying "far out." He baked 93 loaves of whole-grain bread a week for a living, but had never dirtied his hands in a committed relationship. Only in dough.

There was a prosperous businessman who'd found his true purpose through wheeling and dealing and scheming.

"I worry I may have lost my soul," he said gazing into my eyes.

He had. I suggested he look elsewhere for it. Not inside of me.

Most of my dates have fallen between the bread baker and the deal-maker. On a first dinner date, one man revealed so much about his ex-wife's favorite sexual posi-

tion and the fiber content in her diet that I felt she was sitting between us and could have passed me the salt. There was an erudite Princeton professor who at the end of our third date was still discussing *Jude the Obscure*. Several lawyers have blended together in my mind into one 39-regular navy pin-striped suit. And too many psychotherapists told me how I *really* felt.

Dating at my age is about "sort ofs," kissing toads and iguanas, and putting Mr. Potato Head together. One's unavailable, the next is unappealing, and the one I'd have clicked with is dead.

This book will not be a Kiss-and-Tell nor a Kiss-and-Puke. It is my take on dating which can be summed up in the following too-true story:

Early in the morning on the day before my wedding to the man from whom I am now divorced, there was a knock at the door of my parents' apartment where I'd been staying in my old bedroom. My mother was already "putting in time" at the beauty parlor. I was still in bed with my hair in rollers contemplating what I thought was to be my last day as a single woman. My father was in the living room doing what he usually does—nothing—so he answered it.

The voice I heard was my great-aunt Sylvia's, who was out of the family loop. My parents and I had been having a hard time deciding at which table to seat her for the wedding dinner. Or even if we should.

"What do you want?" my father asked.

"I want Nancy to have this," she said, "a little good-luck present."

There was silence for several seconds. Dead silence. Then my father said, "I'll take it."

"Wait," I called. I bounced out and poked my rollered-head into the living room, assuming that Aunt Sylvia's good-luck present was something old or new or borrowed or blue in the form of a beautiful gem.

I didn't assume so well.

What Sylvia was standing in our doorway holding—and I swear on my cat's life I'm not lying—was Jell-O. A mold of green Jell-O with fruit cocktail suspended at the top. It wasn't a regular-looking Jell-O mold either. No. The mold Aunt Sylvia appeared with on the morning before My Wedding, (which you should know was not being held at my parents' home in case you're thinking that the wedding supper was "potluck" and guests had been told to bring a favorite dish) was lopsided.

Instinctively, I tilted my head.

Fortunately, Aunt Sylvia didn't see. My father was closing the door in her face.

Throughout that day, in between calling the florist, the caterer, the photographer and the groom to make sure they'd show up, and talking to the butterflies in my stomach, I summoned my family to the kitchen at regular intervals for viewings. Each time I'd make little mold jokes. Each time I'd tilt my head.

That is how I have come to view dating.

Laugh and tilt! Laugh and tilt!

There is no other way.

PART ONE

GETTING THE FIRST DATE

WHAT IS A DATE?

date (dāt), n., v., dat-ed, dat-ing.
(*According to* Webster's)
—a social appointment, engagement, or occasion arranged
beforehand with a person of the opposite sex.

(*According to Kelton*)
—an activity that may or may not be more fun than sticking
razor blades through one's eyes.
—a social or not-so-social appointment between two persons
that leads to one or more of the following: a second appointment, kissing, more than kissing, total bliss, utter despair,
medication, eczema, a deeply philosophical view of life, marriage, or someone else.
—something we will be doing long after the prom unless
someone comes up with a cure.
Ant: sitting home, being dateless.

●

What Is Being "Dateless"?
—having time to get to know yourself
—having time to give yourself a henna rinse and get the ice
out of your freezer
—giggling on the phone about every jerk you've ever dated
—asking yourself why no jerk is calling now that you're
rinsed and defrosted

●

Questions and Answers:

Q. Is being dateless the same as being celibate?
A. No. Some people have dinner and movie dates with no sex. They are often overachieving women with Jewish parents and men with lots of mucus. They tend to date each other. Others have sex without a movie or dinner. They do all the smiling.

Q. What's a bad time to be dateless?
A. The last ten minutes of December 31.

Q. When is it even worse?
A. On the ramp of Noah's Ark.

WHY DATE?

Before you take the plunge, let's weigh the pros and cons.

Why date	*Why not*
1. Your mother will be thrilled.	1. She'll bug you about something else.
2. You'll have a hand to hold during the scary parts of the movies.	2. It might have warts.
3. You'll have someone to laugh with at the funny parts.	3. It's agony if your date doesn't get it.
4. You can wear the clothes you wouldn't wear to vacuum.	4. Vacuum instead. You'll get more accomplished. Especially if you use attachments.
5. You can try out different behaviors.	5. So can your date.
6. You learn a lot about yourself.	6. *Oy!*
7. You confirm your attractiveness to the opposite sex.	7. You confirm your suspicions of the opposite sex.
8. It gets you over your fear of dating.	8. *Nothing* gets you over your fear of dating.
9. You will have something to discuss with your shrink.	9. You won't get into the childhood stuff.
10. You can make your married friends jealous.	10. You'll have to lie a lot.

Why date	*Why not*
11. It beats not dating.	11. Theoretically.
12. You may find someone so you will never have to date again.	

Isn't Number 12 a compelling enough reason to date?

THE PERFECT DATE

What is a perfect date?
1. An oxymoron
2. Most men until you sleep with them
3. The one who doesn't want you.

•

My neighbor, Karen, a fashion designer, tells the following story:

Early in her career, a buyer came into the showroom where she was working and ordered the entire inventory of a particular outfit, a matching knit shirt and top. Karen wrote up the order, pinned the word "Sold" on the outfit, and when the next buyer came in, she told him everything was available except that. They buyer carefully went through the entire line and then turned to Karen.

"*That's* the one I want," he said wistfully, pointing to the one marked "Sold."

The same thing happened with the next buyer.

So Karen got an idea. She removed the "Sold" sign from the first outfit, pinned it to a less promising one, and explained to the next buyer who came in that everything was available except that.

Sure enough. Guess what the buyer wanted.

"Your basic rule in retailing," Karen said. "Everyone wants the dress marked 'Sold.'"

And your basic rule in life.

It's why women are drawn to bad boys. And why guys want women who are booked the next three Saturdays. Everyone wants the dress marked "Sold" because we want what doesn't come easily—what we cannot have.

It's simple. And perverse.

There was more than a ring of truth when I glibly told a friend what was wrong with two men I dated:

One was not available. The other definitely was.

HOW TO MEET POTENTIAL DATES

Looking Inward
Before going out there, you have to go within. Ask yourself: am I *really* ready to date?

On second thought, *don't.*

No sane, thinking person is ever *really* ready to date. Especially when you can find greater solace from far less nerve-wracking activities like shark fishing, hang gliding, and not dating.

Sort of ready will do.

GOING OUT: TRUE STORIES FROM EVERYDAY LIFE

There are opportunities to meet people by simply living your life. Especially if you have one.

And particularly when you're not looking.

I met a man I'll call Robert in a playground in Central Park. He was with his two daughters. I was with my one. *And* my parents.

I noticed him the second we walked in. We eyed each other more than once. I thought he looked pretty hot. My parents found seats together on a bench in the shade, and as I parked myself on another near the tire swing my daughter was on, he approached me.

"Are you sitting or pushing?" he asked.

"Resting," I said.

His eyes were warm and inviting. We introduced ourselves, chatted easily, then before my mother walked over and got into the act, he asked me for my number.

His daughters wondered who I was. He boldly announced, "Nancy, a new friend."

When my daughter asked the same, I whispered, "Robert, I'm not sure."

For two years we were an item. Then one day we were not. My daughter has outgrown playgrounds.

So I'm "not looking" elsewhere.

RINSING AND SPITTING FOR DATES

I haven't always waited for them to reach out. Sometimes I've made the move. I had a crush on my dentist (I'll call him Dr. J). I decided to let him know that I wanted to get beyond rinsing and spitting.

This decision did not come easily. I agonized and obsessed—alone and with my 11 most intimate friends, including three on another coast. I consulted two cabdrivers and the woman sitting behind me at a Broadway show.

I needed encouragement. There were age and religious differences between Dr. J and me. He had become a widower only recently. He *was* my dentist. We had a cordial, long-standing relationship about teeth. Mine. Period.

I had gone to Dr. J after my neighbor, a longtime patient, described him as "expensive, competent, and nice." For a Manhattan professional, that's as good as it gets. I've known too many whom I'd best describe as "expensive, arrogant, and tanned." Dr. J instilled confidence immediately, although at first I hadn't needed extensive work. My major problems of the eighties had not been dental. The hygienist dealt with my tartar and plaque. Then I needed two gold inlays.

I wasn't sure whether Dr. J was simply a good conversationalist, an affable professional, or a bit of a flirt, but as he drilled, took impressions, and put in the "temps," he chatted easily about everything from movies to his children to people's looks. I had written a magazine article on beauty and before the second visit when he fitted my first gold crown, he read it.

Perhaps I was entertaining the normal fantasies that women have about their doctors and dentists, but I had a better time in Dr. J's chair than I do on most of my dates.

"You need that second crown," he reminded me when he finished the first. "Whenever you're ready."

No, I wanted to say. Whenever *you're* ready.

I decided that after he fitted my second crown, I would let him know I enjoyed his company. Only I didn't get a chance. When he finished his work, he disappeared to make a phone call.

I felt bad. Once again, I cataloged all those reasons not to reach out. I even added two more: he probably had an aversion to dating patients, and he must already have at least one female companion anyway.

Then I thought about Bobby Miller.

At my twenty-first high school reunion, Bobby Miller asked me to dance the first slow dance. As we put our arms around each other and began swaying to the music, I felt like a giddy 16-year-old. In high school, Bobby Miller never asked me out. We often smiled or spoke in passing and sometimes we would be at the same parties, but he always had a girlfriend. Everybody liked Bobby Miller.

In the fifth grade, he sent me a valentine—my first from a boy. I remember thanking him but saying nothing more.

"Do you remember sending me a valentine?" I asked at the reunion. He nodded.

"For months I slept with it under my pillow," I said. "I had such a crush on you but was too scared to talk to you."

"I wish that you had," he told me, "because I dug you too."

I laughed. We both did. Had I shared my feelings way back then, would we have gone steady in fifth grade? Through junior high? The senior prom? College? To the altar?

Knowing who we were and where we each have been, I doubt Bobby Miller and I would have been holding hands beyond our prepubescence. I can never be sure, though. That first slow dance at the reunion got me thinking about other missed opportunities, the what-if's, and the many Bobby Millers with whom I didn't connect from fifth grade on.

Fear. The primary reason we do and fail to do many things in our lives. It's that simple. And that complex.

I dialed Dr. J's office number one day at lunchtime. He answered his own phone. I told him I was planning on dropping off a check for my second gold inlay that afternoon and would like to speak with him then.

When I arrived, his dental assistant was beside him in the room, putting instruments in drawers.

I took a deep breath. "I am wondering if you could step out a minute," I said to her, "I'd like to talk to Dr. J alone."

Puzzled, she glanced from me to him in silence, then walked out. "What's going on here?" he asked.

I took another deep breath. "I just wanted to tell you that I like talking to you," I said. "If and when you are interested in socializing, I would love to see you."

He looked at me impassively. I have no idea whether he was stunned, shocked, touched, flattered, or totally put off by my boldness. "Thanks," he said. "I have your number."

He never called. No matter now. Whatever turned me on back then ceased to exist with time. Still, walking through that door and saying what I wanted was a daring move for me. I was glad I pulled it off.

"You should be," said a friend. "You really stuck your neck out. What could be more terrifying?"

Just one thing. Never having tried.

●

Dentally speaking, I wasn't done. My daughter needed braces. I got the names of two neighborhood orthodontists. One was supposedly terrific. The other was divorced. I figured so what if her teeth grow in crooked and made an appointment with the second.

We had an initial consultation. He told us her teeth were not ready. We should see him again in six months.

I remained silent with my less-than-professional opinion: I found him appealing. My teeth and I could be ready sooner. Six months was a long time to wait.

As luck would have it, I was writing an article involving interviews with professional males. I called and asked if he'd be interested and he said, "Over dinner, on me."

Guess who asked the first question.

"Are you seeing anyone?" he wanted to know.

"That's not part of the interview," I told him. "Are you?"

He nodded. He had a longtime steady girlfriend. What did I have in mind?

"The interview." I turned on my tape recorder and proceeded.

Nothing more about "us."

Six months later, he wired up my daughter's mouth. Three years later he took the braces off. Her smile is now gorgeous. Her overbite is gone.

And I've pretty much had it with "teeth" men.

10 OFFBEAT WAYS TO MEET PEOPLE

Every place is a potential meeting ground if you think creatively. Here are 10 offbeat ways:

1. Go to AA or other Anonymous meetings even if you are not in recovery.
So many people are.

2. Go to employment agencies even if you have a job.
So many people don't.

3. Get stuck in traffic.
This will not work if you live in a rural area and the only other thing on the road is a cow.
Go out of your way to get stuck in the kind of bottleneck traffic that would give people who aren't looking for dates a stroke. Then instead of cursing, honking, and snarling, flirt, with everyone who isn't with his mother.

4. Get stuck in traffic in New Jersey
Do all of the above plus take deep breaths. You will be in simpatico with other "stuck" drivers, who are also holding their noses and saying "pee-eew."

5. Talk to people in the waiting rooms of professionals.
Your dentist's, doctor's, vet's, and accountant's offices are fertile meeting grounds. Skip your lawyer's. Seeing him is enough for one day. You are not at your best.
On second thought, go *straight* to your lawyer's. If another client is as disgruntled as you are, you two might bond as quickly as "stuck" drivers in New Jersey.
Stench is stench.

6. If you are a woman, answer ads to buy a Mercedes, a BMW, a Porsche, or any other car even if you don't drive.
You may want the seller.

7. If you are a woman, answer ads to buy a boat even if you don't row.
Ditto.

8. Go to your friends' high school and college reunions.
Have them introduce you to *everyone*, especially those who were "most likely to succeed."

9. Go to your friends' family parties.
Skip your own family gatherings. You *know* those people. You know how they make you feel about *still* being single year after year.

10. Attend funerals.
Not of strangers, although if you look great in black, it's not a terrible idea, but of relatives, friends' relatives, and relatives' friends.

Don't feel guilty about acting on this suggestion. Despite what your mother may have told you, your marital status is *not* a leading cause of death.

So pay your respects. And pay them in smart, nicely tailored clothes. Subtly look around the reception area and the chapel. See who is unattached.

And alive.

If someone interests you before or after the service, strike up a simple, brief conversation indicating in a respectful way that it would be nice to talk again in the absence of a casket.

Years ago, at a close friend's mother-in-law's funeral, I met a man. Not just a man. A doctor. Not just a doctor either. An orthopedic surgeon.

It was the Sunday morning of Daylight Savings Time and I had arrived an hour early, because I'd forgotten to turn back my clock. He arrived early, I suspect, to meet women. We talked. He asked me if I'd like to get together sometime.

"Out of respect for Mrs. Miller, I don't think this is the best time to discuss it," I said.

My friend, standing nearby and eavesdropping, came over and pulled me aside.

"What are you? Demented?" she whispered. "It's a perfect time. Give him your number. He's a doctor, you jerk. My mother-in-law would be thrilled."

I went out with the orthopedic surgeon the following Friday. I couldn't say I had a swell time. I couldn't even say I had fun. What I might call our Friday evening, which ended at 10:30 with my stomach growling from starvation because he was too cheap and too-a-whole-lot-of-other-things-which-I-can't-get-into-here to take me for a milkshake, let alone a meal, was a *date from the depths of hell.*

No harm, though. No harm at all. I was open. I went for it. And I know from experience—the good and the bad—that things do happen in the strangest ways in the most unlikely places when we are least expecting them.

There'll be other funerals.

DATING ANONYMOUS

A one-time colleague, whom I'll call Ted, told me the story I'm about to share with you:

She was sitting toward the back of an AA meeting at a neighborhood church when I walked in. Our eyes met. We smiled. It was "Some Enchanted 12-Step Evening."

We glanced at each other several times and afterward she lingered at the door until I came out, then with another sweet glance, signaled she was interested.

We introduced ourselves. Her name is Michelle. As luck would have it, we live a few blocks apart. She mentioned that she thought she'd seen me in the supermarket and bank. I was really flattered.

Neither of us mentioned the meeting, the program, or our recovering from alcoholism, which was what we were both supposedly doing. When I asked her for her phone number, she gave it to me.

I didn't understand why, then, when I called her the next day and asked her out, she was very curt. She said she wouldn't be available after all, because something came up. She didn't say what.

That evening, I went to an Overeaters' Anonymous meeting in the same room at the church. I arrived early and sat up front. The leader, seeing I was a newcomer, asked if I might like to introduce myself and "share" why I was there.

I told him I might not.

What would I have said? That I wasn't really an overeater, but an underdater and was there to meet women?

As I walked out afterward, guess who was sitting alone in the back row? Michelle. We smiled. She blushed. Neither of us said a word about the meeting, the program, overeating, or her blowing me off on the phone. I asked her if she'd like to go for a cup of decaf or tea.

She shook her head.

"We won't eat anything," I said with a little chuckle. Considering we'd just attended an Overeaters' Anonymous Meeting, I thought that was pretty cute.

Michelle didn't think it was cute at all. She told me she had to be somewhere.

"Michelle," I called. "Please, can we talk?"

But no, she was out of there. Fast.

The next night my choices were Gamblers' Anonymous and Al-Anon. I decided against GA. My cousin Arnie would be there.

I got to the Al-Anon meeting very, very late. As I sat down all the way in the back, a woman in the front volunteered to stand up and "share."

Oh my God!

It was Michelle.

"Hi, my name is Michelle," she said, "and I'm here because of a man."

A few people clapped. A woman sitting near me mumbled to the one beside her, "Aren't we all?"

Michelle went on. "He's not someone I'm seeing, but I've noticed him around in the neighborhood. I've had a crush on him and I wanted to figure out how we could meet.

My heart started racing. Michelle went on.

"One night I saw him at the supermarket and decided to make my move. I got scared. I followed him in my car. At least I'd see where he lived.

"He didn't go home. He went to an AA meeting. I went, too. We talked. I thought he was really neat. I gave him my number, then I got cold feet. My ex-husband is an alcoholic. Not a recovering one, either. A mean, abusive one. No way could I do that again.

"The next night I was driving home and saw this guy's car in front of the church again. I went in. An OA meeting was in session. He was there.

"I knew I made the right decision not to go out with him. I mean, AA *and* OA. Yet I can't stop thinking about him." Michelle paused, then went on. "Something tells me he's not really such a mess."

I started clapping liked I'd never clapped before. People turned to look at me. They started clapping, too. Michelle saw me and went rushing out of the room.

I wanted to call out, "Michelle, I can explain."

I wanted to run to her side, pick her up, and carry her out of the meeting, the way Richard Gere carried Debra Winger out of the factory in *An Officer and a Gentleman.*

But this was not Hollywood. It was Al-Anon. Not that there's any difference.

The meeting ended. The Bingo people were waiting to get in. Bingo is held at 8:00 every evening after our Anonymous meetings.

When I got outside, there was Michelle, smiling at me like she'd done that first night after AA. I walked over to her and for the first time in my life, I told a woman the whole truth. That I was attending Anonymous meetings with the hope of meeting someone. She was shocked. Not as shocked as I had been when she'd announced she had a crush on me.

We went out for a drink and talked for three hours. The next night we went out for dinner. And the next. And the next. And the next.

That was a year ago. We've been together ever since. Not overdrinking or overeating. Or overattending meetings.

We're enjoying life to the fullest. Together and Anonymous.

ASK THE DATING SHRINK

Dear Dating Shrink:

I recently attended a funeral. The deceased was the mother of one of my thirteen-year-old son's classmates. I didn't know the woman very well.

Actually, I didn't know her at all.

I shook the new widower's hand, anyway, and said, "I'm very sorry."

"Who are you?" asked the grief-stricken man.

"Ben's mother," I told him. I wondered if he noticed my new belt.

"Who's Ben?" he said.

George, his son, was standing beside him. "Ben's on the soccer team with me."

"Oh," was all the widower said. Maybe my dress with the jacket would have looked better.

I got a printed thank you card from the family. That was it.

Can you think of another way for me to pursue George's father?

Signed: Not Bad in Black

Dear N.B.I.B.

Yes. Call and suggest attending a soccer game together.

Dating Shrink

Dear Shrink,

The soccer season is over. Now what?

N.B.I.B.

Dear N.B.I.B.

See if there's something else you can watch together as parents. What else do your sons both do?

Dating Shrink

Dear D.S.

Pick their pimples and, I assume, masturbate. Any more suggestions?

N.B.I.B.

Dear N.B.I.B.

Not with George's father, but since you have got the *chutzpah* and the outfit to attend strangers' funerals, call some undertakers and get on their mailing lists.

Dating Shrink

BLIND AND
VERY BLIND DATES

Like the new celibacy and the old impotency, they're not going anywhere, so we might as well deal with them.

●

blind date, (blind dāt), n.
—a social appointment between a man and a woman arranged by a third person, who gives each participant a glowing yet untruthful earful about the other.
—a social engagement that is more dreaded than standardized tests.

very blind date, (ver ē blind dāt), n.
—all of the above but *worse.*

●

The matchmaker is usually a friend or someone who claims to be your friend, but it can also be:
—your friends' friends;
—your parents' friends;
—the piano tuner;
—your chiropractor;
—your aerobics instructor, coworkers, bus driver, dry cleaner, and all the people to whom you regularly *kvetch;*
—your father;
—his broker;
—your mother;
—her hair-colorist;
—her canasta club;
—the canasta club's hair-colorists;
—*everyone who knows you're looking.*

TIPS FOR SURVIVING BLIND AND VERY BLIND DATES

Enjoying blind and very blind dates is tricky. Surviving them is a more realistic goal. The following tips might help:

1. Without whining or sounding like you haven't had a date since Steve and Edie started singing together even if it's true, let everyone on the previous page know you would like to be fixed up.

2. Let *everyone* except for hardened criminals know.

3. Actually, let hardened criminals know too. They may have friends, relatives, and ghostwriters who are law-abiding and *single*.

4. Expect *nothing*. Remember: most people's first obligation is to fix up their unattached relatives and closer, more pathetic friends.

5. If someone does fix you up, and the date is decent or better, don't get too excited. Most dates, like milk, eventually turn sour.

6. If the date is good to terrific, take it in stride and remember: a good blind date is one of life's little surprises.

7. Forget little surprises. A good blind date is a miracle.

8. Remember though: It *can* happen. It might. It has.

●

A *Blind Date that Lasted:*

"What were you going to do tonight before I called?" my father asked my mother. The year was 1932.

That question, she says, "got" her. So did his voice. With their friends, Agnes and Ed, who fixed them up, they went out that very evening.

And clicked.

The four years that they dated consisted of their sitting at my mother's house listening to my grandmother and the relatives mumble, "So when?"

My father claims he never asked for her hand in marriage, but one day just found himself standing beside her with all their relatives in the room, and heard her say, "I do."

That was in 1936.

"There was something about him I liked as soon as I heard his voice," is how my mother tells it whenever I ask about that first phone call.

And now after 63 years of hearing that voice, that "something" is still there.

●

A *Blind Date that Never Should Have Happened:*

This one was not mine. I heard it from a friend.

She knew someone who, on a *very blind* lunch date, sensed in a half a second that the man was totally "off." He was unable to smile or make eye contact. There was nothing resembling "vibes." Throughout the meal, he answered her in grunts and monosyllables while looking at his watch.

The best, she claimed, she could hope for was that her food go down the right pipe. Yet when lunch was over, he gave her a huge smile, a long handshake, and said with great earnestness, "I can't thank you enough."

"Really?" she said. "For what?"

"My buddy bet me I was incapable of sitting through an entire meal with an ugly woman," he told her. "He's waiting in the car for me. Now I can go and collect."

BRING·A·MAN AND OTHER PARTIES

party—par•ty (pärt•ē)
(*According to* Webster's)
—n. 1. a social gathering, as of invited guests at a private home, for conversation, refreshments, entertainment, etc.: a cocktail party.
2. a group gathered for some special purpose or task: a fishing party, a search party.

(*According to Kelton*)
—n. 1. a social gathering for conversation, refreshments, entertainment, and finding out:
  a. who is eligible
  b. who, among the couples, is splitting up and becoming eligible
  c. who, among any guests—single or otherwise—can drive us home and soon.
2. a group gathered for the purpose of making single people:
  a. wish they were somewhere—anywhere—else
  b. sorry they ever dumped their mates

•

To meet people at parties, you have to get invited. And show. Wearing an "Open For Business" sign.

I was invited to a party a few months after my marriage ended and didn't want to go. My eyes were still bloodshot. My wounds were too raw.

"You have to start somewhere," a friend said.

The little voice inside me did too.

I went. So did twentysome women and a half a dozen men. (It's the same at every party, in every state, in every decade.) The first one I spoke to was a Hebrew calligrapher. He thought it was neat that we were *both* writers. I thought two thousand years ago, he'd have been a good catch. Three other female guests obviously felt differently. They got into our conversation, and asked *him* about *his* pens.

I then smiled at a high-waisted guy who looked like he'd smile back. He did. I approached him. We talked. He asked me out for dinner for the following Saturday.

My first postmarital date.

The good news was that he'd gone to college in my hometown, Buffalo, so we had two sure-fire topics: chicken wings and snow. The bad news was that he was significantly younger and nerdier than I had thought.

"This is nothing personal, but the baby-sitter told me she had to leave by eleven," I said when I saw deep nerdiness kick in.

I was happy that he bought it. And happier that he stopped at a Korean grocers and bought scallions.

"What do you need those for?" I asked.

"Tuna salad. Don't you put scallions in tuna?"

I hadn't, but I bought a bunch that evening and chopped them into my tuna the very next day. Yum!

There's something to be learned from everyone.

•

I was surprised when my neighbor, Lulu, invited me to a party.

Lulu is a hooker. We'd often chat in the early evening when we'd both be leaving for work: I'd be carrying folders with my writing students' manuscripts. She'd be in gold lamé.

"So Friday night, you'll come?" she said.

It was between *that* and not sleeping.

At the designated hour, I rang her bell.

It was the first time I'd been inside Lulu's apartment. And world. It was a toss-up which made me feel more out of place: not wearing a skin-tight, metallic jumpsuit or not being buddies with the pimps.

The men had slicked-back hair, pinky rings, and huge cigars. They looked like friends of Nathan Detroit's. The women were in boas, sequins, and silver or gold outfits that left nothing to the imagination. It was *Irma la Douce, The Best Little Whorehouse in Texas,* and *Guys and Dolls* all rolled into one. Without a score. Or lyrics. Or talent.

In my cable-knit crew neck sweater and wool slacks, I looked a wee bit "preppy." At most parties, I can get a conversation going with someone. At Lulu's, I couldn't connect with the dip.

The only icebreaker that came to mind was: "How's tricks?"

No one noticed when I left.

•

Bring-a-Man Parties:

In the late eighties, I was "networked" by a woman I'll call Beth, who got my name from a friend. She was hosting something I'll call "bring-a-man parties" and invited me to her office to hear about the particulars.

I arrived at her midtown, 37th-floor office in the sky at the designated time. Two other bring-a-man recruits were already seated in the reception area. One wore fake clear nails, too much makeup, and costume jewelry. The other had on a dark mink. A third designer-dressed, beautifully-accessorized, bring-a-man candidate got off the elevator and joined us.

"Are you here about the party?" she asked us.

We nodded. There was no sign of Beth, whom none of us knew. For the next fifteen minutes we made small talk. Very small. Mostly about how Beth found us and where we lived. The three of them were within walking distance of the Ralph Lauren store. I'd been bused in from downtown.

Beth appeared. She had unkempt blond hair that was very bleached, black stretch pants that were very, very tight, a vacuous-looking face with no smile or character, and a cold, limp handshake that pretty much said it all.

She ushered us into her office and we pulled up chairs around her desk. On it was something that looked like a scrapbook. The woman wearing the dead animal mumbled, "There's the book."

Beth sat down and without any eye contact began.

"The parties are at an uptown apartment, of course. Your admission ticket is a male escort who earns $250,000 or more. If he's . . ."

I raised my hand. "$250,000?"

"Right." Beth went on, "If he's over 50, he's got to be great looking. Under 50, decent'll do."

The uptown gals had no questions. They were all eyeing "The Book."

"The Book" contained the names, addresses, and occupations of men who'd already attended Beth's parties, along with the names of the women who'd brought them. Underneath were comments and ratings for each, and how much the men earned.

"How do you know?" I asked.

Beth smiled. "After each party, the women write reports."

"No, I mean how much the men make," I said.

The accessorized woman looked at me like I'd arrived from Planet Mars.

Beth's smile faded. "I run these parties for one reason: to have hundreds of wealthy men paraded before me. Obviously, I do a credit check on each."

Beth was serious. The other women were, too. They opened "The Book" and started going through it, discussing the men they knew.

I recognized one name. He was a Harvard attorney/ businessman who wore a Rolex, an Armani, and a sneer. And he'd worn them all with me. We dated one summer. My being a "downtown writer" initially intrigued him as his nouveau polish did me. A porcupine would have been easier to get close to, though. The ice in his veins did not melt. He returned to his world of form and appearances with his labels and his sneer.

I didn't share my comments about him with this crew. He was close in proximity and soul to them and to the Ralph store. To them, he'd be a catch.

Beth continued, "The parties are on Tuesdays. The second Tuesday of each month."

I burst out, "I can't come." Silently, I started thanking God.

"Why not?" asked the lady in too-much-of-everything.

"I teach Tuesday evenings."

"Teach?" Beth said. "So switch your class to another evening or get a sub."

"No." I stood up. "Teaching's my work. Like this is yours."

I extended my hand to Beth's. Her handshake was limp like before. The woman in the dead animal looked at me like I'd just farted in her elevator.

I said good-bye to this bring-a-man crew as they continued leafing through "The Book of Beth's Credit-Checked Men."

●

Nine Things I've Learned at Parties:
1. You can't connect with everyone.
2. I'm not so great with credit-checked men.
3. Or uptown gals and pimps.
4. In large groups, women outnumber men (except in jails and soup kitchens).
5. It's easy to meet someone if you're clear and focused.
6. And male.
7. If you aren't, it helps to have chutzpah.
8. Tuna tastes better with scallions.
9. There's something to be learned from *everyone,* including high-waisted men.

AVOIDING DIRT:
DECODING THE PERSONALS

The personals are popular for people who are not. They are also great for people who have:
—little contact in their daily lives with the opposite sex
—little contact with reality
—lots of contact but little going for them.

●

There is good and bad news about the personals.

Good	*Bad*
1. you increase your pool of pickings	1. you get an ocean of dorks
2. you get a clear idea of what you want	2. and a clearer idea of what's out there.

●

The following matching exercise will give you a clue to what is and is not said in the personals.

1. Where to place an ad if you've heard of Susan Sontag.
2. What women *never* mention they have.
3. What you can tell about a person from his or her ad.
4. What men say they want.
5. What men *really* want.

Choose from this list:
—oral sex
—The *New York Review of Books*
—a woman who enjoys hiking, biking, sharing, laughing, and opera
—absolutely nothing
—superfluous facial hair

Answers:
1. The *New York Review of Books*
2. superfluous facial hair
3. absolutely nothing
4. A woman who enjoys hiking, biking, sharing, laughing, and opera
5. oral sex

●

When I was a small child, my family and two others went to a resort together. It was a new resort. No one we knew had been there, but it was exactly what we wanted.

According to the brochure.

The full-colored pictures were breathtaking. The facilities were impressive. Especially the Olympic-size pool.

That was the clincher.

All seven kids loved the water. A few were serious swimmers. One was on her school team. Another was taking lifesaving. The youngest had just learned to dog-paddle without his tube and couldn't wait to show off his stuff.

"Where's the pool?" our little dog-paddler asked the desk clerk as our parents were checking in.

The desk clerk gave us a funny look. "Pool? What pool?"

"This one," I said, opening a brochure on the desk and pointing to the picture of the beautiful Olympic-size pool, relieved that it was there.

"Oh. Right." The desk clerk chuckled. "It'll be that way," he said, pointing to the sliding glass doors at the end of the lobby which led outside. "It's not built yet, but you can go see where they're digging."

We looked at the brochure. Closely. Very, very closely. At the bottom of the page, in print so fine one could barely see it without a magnifying glass, it said: "Plans for our pool now under way. To be finished next year."

And yes! There outside through the sliding glass doors at the end of the lobby was an Olympic-size hole surrounded by mounds and mounds of dirt.

●

If you wish to be in the pool swimming and not stuck with mounds of dirt, *read*. Carefully. Between the lines and through them.

An ad is an ad.

It's not the *whole* truth, and nothing but the truth.

Everyone lies.

"Not me," claims your date, your friend, or a person you know who just placed ad.

Okay. Maybe "stretches," "twists," "embellishes," "elaborates," "exaggerates," "omits," or "practices denial" would be more like it.

Maybe we should call it putting one's best foot forward.

Or ignoring a blind spot the size of a Buick.

Maybe.

We can call it whatever anyone wants. The truth is: everyone lies.

•

Commonly used personal words and phrases:

a striking blond—If she says she is one and is over the age of 11, what she means is: she has a great hair colorist. If he says he's seeking one, he's shallow, but honest. The only woman who should answer his ad are the ones with great colorists.

enjoys films (not movies)—If she says "films" she probably wears black. If he says "films" he is affected and possibly gay. If they "enjoy films" together, they're not going to have much sex.

aggressive—If he says he's aggressive, he's either Commander-in-Chief of the Armed Forces or a Litigator from Hell. If he hates aggressive women, his last girlfriend had call-waiting and once put him on hold.

a successful professional—If he says he is one, he's probably an accountant, a podiatrist, or a dentist (if he were a doctor or lawyer, he'd say "doctor" or "lawyer," wouldn't he?). If he says he is seeking one, he is either liberated or cheap.

seeking an understanding mate—Who on planet Earth isn't?

•

A Cautionary Tale:

I have a cousin—54 and divorced—whom I'll call Princess. She wasn't looking for the Prince, mind you, but when she just happened to see the following, she knew he was looking for her:

> SWM*—distinguished gentleman 50 seeks "real" relationship with a classy, younger woman who appreciates life's little treasures: good conversation, long walks, my yacht, my home in St. Barts, expensive jewelry, and expensive everything else. Must share my love of fancy dining and dressing.**

Princess ran for her Gold Cross pen and Crane's notepaper and without a word about her tummy tuck, breast implant, or facelift, she wrote a one-page letter describing her "realness."

The distinguished SWM called. He let her know he was a CEO*** of an NEC**** and was WCPAS*****. Princess's newly-raised jaw dropped and when the SWM invited her

---

* SWM, as most people know, is Single White Male

** Not herbal or blue cheese or creamy Italian, but expensive, chic, well-tailored, designer, and custom-made clothing

*** Chief Executive Officer

**** Nauseatingly Enormous Company

***** Well Connected Politically and Socially

to dine at his favorite four-star restaurant, Princess said, "I'd better check my appointment book."

SWM waited while Princess checked.

"That'll be fine," she then said, not mentioning that every other night for the rest of her life would be just fine, too.

SWM arrived for their date wearing a VVECMS.******

Princess offered him a drink. He shook his head and smiled a big one. "We'll have my favorite wine with dinner, but that's later. Much later." He glanced around her living room. "Your place is lovely, but not as lovely as you. We're going to kiss now, get naked and shower, then take it from there." He pulled her close and started to put his lips on hers.

Princess pushed him away. "We've hardly spoken."

"Right," he said, coming toward her again.

"Or eaten," Princess said, pushing him across the room. There were no more royal words between them.

Prince was out the door.

Eight points to ponder from the above example:
1. there's no such thing as free lunch or dinner
2. or free anything
3. a first meeting with a stranger should be in a public place no matter who has a castle or a pedigree
4. the Prince is getting lousy press
5. he deserves it
6. most princes love dressing, but not as much as undressing
7. a princess still thinks *he* is the answer
8. whether she is plastic or real.

****** Very, Very Expensive Custom-Made Suit

Okay. So the jerks of the century are out there. But so are some pretty swell folks. And we've all heard the phrase: water finds its own level.

We're just not sure what it means.

Write the following and you'll be guaranteed a huge response.

If you are a female:
Very pretty, very fit woman seeks man for anything but a commitment.

If you are a male:
SWM with great sense of humor, feelings, successful career, ivy education, and feelings about those
feelings seeks female counterpart for sharing, car-
ing, talking, walking, and commitment.

So will this:
SWM with job and pulse.

And this:
SWM.

●

My friend, a college English professor, had been search-
ing for her "intellectual match." She salivated when she
read the following:
Stimulating, bookish Ph.D. in literature seeks
Brontë's Jane and Flaubert's Emma. Our minds
should meet.

What happened:
My friend, Ms. Intellect, responded with a brief but
eloquent letter. Mr. Lit. called her immediately. Their
minds met. Their bodies, however, remained in different
time zones. Towards the end of their fourth date, he was
still discussing *Beowulf.*

Ms. Intellect's Marianne Williamson's–boosted self-esteem went flying out the window. Suddenly she saw herself as the ugliest, most sexless creature on this planet. She asked Mr. Lit. why he was so aloof. He said he wasn't aloof at all, but that she was excessively female and demanding.

●

What the Dating Shrink says really happened:

Mr. Lit thinks he is stimulating and bookish. The truth is: Mr. Lit. is boring, prissy, and probably gay.

The cerebral stuff is heady. At first.

Then Ms. Intellect wants a kiss. Or a hand to hold. Something more than his words.

And Mr. Lit. can't give it. Or won't.

Ms. Intellect is quietly raging, seriously horny, and longing for affection.

Because when it comes to men and women, it's *not* about words at all.

●

When placing an ad, it's good if you are clear. And better if you're sane. The following ad did not get a single response:

> Seeking: a nondescript, nonentity of a daughter-in-law unlike my first, a slob, or my second, the Bitch.
> My son, Norman, stutters. Especially around me.
> And I *am* around.

The following appeared in the same magazine two weeks later:

> SWM desperately seeking hit man to do away with Mom. Photo not essential. Lethal weapon is.

Norman's mother is more alive than ever. The first "hit man" couldn't bump her off. He was smitten so he took her to dinner instead.

Before their entrées arrived, he explained what he'd been hired to do. Mom got Norman's point. And his hired gun, too. They're deeply in love and a psychopathic team. And Norman stopped stuttering and found love on his own.

●

Nine points that can (but probably won't) be learned from this tale about Norman and his mother:
1. Love comes when you are not looking
2. Especially if you're a lunatic
3. The best way to meet people is to be yourself
4. Unless you're anything like Norman
5. Nothing ever turns out as planned
6. You don't die from being a total pain in the ass
7. Overbearing mothers, like everyone, benefit from love
8. *There is someone out there for everyone*
9. See #2.

●

Years ago, I went out with a shrink. Years ago I went out with many shrinks. Each was screwier than the last.

The shrink I'm about to tell you about—Dave, I'll call him—was a fellow jogger who I met on the track at my gym. He asked me out shortly after I'd stopped seeing Robert.

"You're very quiet," Dave said when he picked me up for our date.

True. I'd found him more attractive sweating.

"You seem a little down," Dave said.

And getting even downer.

"Don't you think it would be a good idea to discuss your feelings?" he asked.

It was the first time in my life I didn't.

"See if you can share your feelings with me now," he said, rolling his hand the way shrinks learned to roll their hands at shrink school or from watching Bob Newhart as a television shrink in the seventies.

"I don't think that would be such a swell idea."

"I do."

"Okay," I said, taking a deep breath. "I'm totally turned off. I hate being analyzed. I miss the guy I recently broke up with. I didn't realize how much until now."

Dave nodded. "It's good that you can say that.

It was better that he took me home.

Dave checked in regularly. To see if I was up to snuff and ready to go out.

I was, but not with him.

He said he was looking for a relationship that lasted beyond the psychoanalytical hour. If we weren't going to see each other, could I tell him what I thought of his ad. It read:

> Very successful clinical psychologist mid-thirties
> with Ph.D., solid practice, great sense of humor
> seeks bright, caring kindred soul (26–40) for mar-
> riage, children, and more.

I thought Dave sounded fabulous. On paper. They *all* do. And that "great sense of humor" was pushing it just a tad. All men think they have a great sense of humor. All men think they are good drivers and good lovers, too.

I told him not to change a thing. Every woman and her mother who reads his ad will respond. I would, too, if I didn't know Dave.

He put it in a magazine just as it was—sense of humor and all—and got the kind of response that a man with a profession and a penis would expect.

Hundreds and hundreds of letters.

Dave sorted through them between psychoanalytical hours. He went out with three women. The third, Enid, a psychotherapist, was "It."

He knew as soon as they spoke. He was sure on their first date.

Enid and Dave have been married for five years. They have adjoining offices on West End Avenue where they simultaneously nod. And in between their psychoanalytical hours, they ask each other how they feel.

I've seen them socially on several occasions. Around them, I feel "well."

•

What I learned from Dave and his ad:
—If you're clear about what you want, you'll get it.
—Especially if you're a white male with a profession and a penis that goes up.*
—Shrinks belong together.
—And not with anyone else.
—It's definitely possible to meet your life's mate through the personals.
—And live simultaneously ever after.

* Dave and Enid have kids.

RULES FOR A FIRST DATE

You don't know much about the other person. You don't know what to expect. Embarking on this new venture can be really exciting.

It usually isn't.

Here are five rules to help you through the early stages without perspiration or Thorazine:

Rule	*Reasons to Follow*	*When to Break*
Rule 1—Do more listening than talking.	People *love* to talk about themselves.	If he is an Orator from Hell.
	You'll bring the other person out.	If you've brought the other person too far out.
Rule 2—Do not immediately think "This is it."	It usually isn't. You'll see skid marks.	Don't.
Rule 3—Do not take your date's behavior personally.	If the other person is arrogant, ambivalent, selfish, cheap, surly, or in another time zone, he or she was like that long before you came along.	If *all* your dates are arrogant, ambivalent, selfish, cheap, surly, and in another time zone, take it *very, very,* personally. Something's radically wrong with your picking process!
Rule 4—Trust your gut.	It's the only truth you've got.	Never!

Rule 1: The Listening Rule

There is listening. And there is listening. You'd know what I am talking about if you've ever dated a lawyer.

Or a Mel.

Mel is a marketing consultant and I should have known at the beginning of our first date when I casually asked about his career and he not so casually replied that it is comprised of three components—research, lecturing, and his private consulting, which he then explained to me, along with how he has structured his work life for the last two decades—that instead of listening, smiling, acting interested, and accepting a second date, I should have said I was really a man. (I actually considered it, but had a hunch that he'd like me better.)

But no. I went out with him again and as soon as opened the door, I shut my mouth. Or else we'd have been a duet.

Fortunately, my veal marsala was more palatable than Mel's two-course story about some colleague who had no connection to me or to us, not that we had a connection. After swallowing my last bite, I wiped my mouth and asked, "Does your colleague have a pink bathroom?"

I'd just had my bathroom painted pink the day before and when I showed it to Mel earlier, he stopped orating a second to say "uh huh."

"What on earth does a pink bathroom have to do with anything?" Mel asked. His eyes were on me now. He noticed I was there.

"Nothing," I said. "It has absolutely nothing to do with anything." My voice was quivering. "I wanted your attention. I'd like to talk, too."

"So you're telling me I'm an old windbag," Mel said.

"Oh no." Finally, finally, Mel was precise.

I stood up and put on my blazer. "If you're considering dessert, the cannolis are great here."

For the first and only time in my life, I walked out on a date.

Rule 2: "This is it."
What typically happens with the people we date?
1. Nothing
2. Something

1. Nothing: This is definitely not *it.*
   When things are off at the starting gate, the following variations of "this is it" leap to mind:
—This is pathetic.
—This is worse than the last one.

2. Something: This is it!
   What in life is more exciting than a promising start? (Great sex, but this book is about dating.) Instead of thinking "this is *it,*" try:
—This is fun.
—This is something.
—This could lead to something.
—This has potential.
—This is definitely better than the last one.

   I met a man on vacation. It was an "across a crowded hotel dining room" thing. He'd just arrived. I was about to leave. I had to work real fast.
   His smile exploded. My insides did too. He lived an hour away from New York. As soon as his vacation ended, we started going out.
   That he was as swept away as I was made me giddy to no end. In high school, his type had no clue I lived and breathed. Obviously, I'd gotten more appealing with age.
   And stupider.
   Because we only got together on my turf, and when I wanted to see where he lived, he said that wouldn't be possible.
   "How come?"
   "Something's there that'll upset you."
   "Roaches?" What else, I wondered. His mother was dead.
   "A woman."
   Nothing came out of my mouth.

He must have thought I didn't "get it" because he then said, "My girlfriend."

I got it. It stung. I swore I'd never think "this is *it*" again.

And I didn't. Until the next time.

Rule 3: Do Not Personalize

We are who we are long before "the date."

The guy who almost made me think that he was ordering one Jack Daniel's after another because new people made him nervous didn't just happen to find "the bar" after he rang my bell.

And the one with very deep pockets who asked me to meet him at a restaurant at 7:30, then told me my choices—a drink *or* dessert—did not just become the cheapest creep on the face of the earth that evening at 7:29.

●

Men think I repeat myself just to annoy them. For example, if someone says "no" when I offer a drink, I invariably ask again. And no matter what it is on the table for discussion, I give my opinion more than once.

The reasons are deep-seated and not at all about *him*.

I repeat myself. I repeat myself.

It's one flaw I bring to dates.

Rule 4: Trust Your Gut

Our gut is our truth. In dating. And in life.

If he looks like a rat, he's probably a rat. And if you don't get a whiff of his testosterone, there's probably not much there.

When someone gets you at primal level, he can say or wear whatever he likes, including an aqua flowered shirt. If someone doesn't turn you on, his flowered shirt will make you puke.

PART TWO

"I'LL CALL YOU"

"I'LL CALL YOU"

"I'll call you" is what a man says to a woman on parting whether they had sparks or a snooze.

•

To her "I'll call you" means I'll call you. The second he leaves no matter what time it is, she starts staring at the phone.

To him "I'll call you" means:
—I'll call you if I don't find a "10."
—what a woman's "It's okay" means when he is a dud in bed.
—you'll hear from me sometime between tomorrow and a year from next July.
—you'll hear from me after the playoffs.
—you'll never hear from me again.
—I'll call you if I don't lose interest, your number, or my nerve.

RUDE AWAKENINGS

Epiphanies aren't always obvious. Sometimes it takes several dates, weeks, or months into a perking romance before you see that you could never contemplate a future with this person. Or even much of a present.

Pay attention to the following telltale signs:
—how he plays games
—how he lives
—how he looks at you
—how he makes love.

1. How he plays games:

A mensch is a mensch. A wimp is a wimp and a son-of-a-bitch is a son-of-a-bitch whether you're keeping score or not.

My friend, Bonnie, once played Scrabble with a shark of an attorney who gloated over his every word and raised objections to hers. He won—not by masterful playing but by bullying, intimidation, and cross-examining her to tears. When they were done, he actually asked if she'd like to see him again.

She told him, "Only if I'm sued."

2. How he lives:

The following in men's houses have turned me on or off:

Turn On	Turn Off
It was him. I could feel him everywhere.	His mother. Her taste was everywhere. So was she.
Lasagna pans, cooking utensils, and tons of food in the frig, including leftovers wrapped in foil.	The only time he used his kitchen was to get from the alcove to the john.
Lots of interesting photos of family, friends, and trips.	The only photograph anywhere was one of his two maiden aunts.
House plants, fresh-cut flowers, pets, *tchotchkes,* and other evidence of life, including lovely children from a previous marriage who are only there part-time.	Artificial flowers, artificial *anything.*
Lots of interesting reading material.	Total turn-off: Leonard Saginbaum's house (see next page).

I could deal with his living in Split-Level Town, Long Island (sort of). And that the "decorator-picked" furniture matched the "decorator-picked" artwork, frames, and accessories, including a china poodle sitting on the living room floor just begging to be smashed (not really).

What I couldn't stomach was seeing beautiful, floor-to-ceiling bookshelves with nothing—absolutely nothing—on them.

"Where do you keep your books?" I asked, staring at the emptiness.

"I don't have any," he said.

He didn't. Not even a cookbook. Or a paperback copy of *The Firm*. I'd have settled for any trace of evidence that Leonard Saginbaum had an interior life, a personality, or a soul.

3. How he looks at you:
a. with jaundiced eyes—if they're tinged with prejudice, hostility, or anything other than kindness and respect, run. You need him like you need a twin-kidney ailment.
b. with lust—if he sees you "that way," enjoy it. Especially if you see him that way, too. If "lust" is *all* that's in his eyes, though, lust may be all you'll get.
c. with a "vacancy" sign—if there's no signs of life or

intelligence in his eyes, he's either a do-do bird, dead, or a good substitute for a sleeping pill.

4. Avoiding eye contact:
If he can't hold your gaze, it might mean that he:
a. is on Lithium
b. is on illegal drugs
c. is on a. and b.
d. has run out of a. *and* b.
e. finds you unappealing
f. can't get it up
g. can't keep it up
h. can't connect with another person for deep-seated, complex reasons which you can't pretend to understand (but have *everything* to do with his mother).

5. How he makes love:
Having sex with a new person is scarier than public speaking. (Except for U.S. presidents. They seem to breeze through both.) The first time can be fabulous. More likely it's a whole lot less. Not counting the following external problems:
1. an earthquake
2. children, parents, or the exterminator showing up unexpectedly
3. one or both partners has a heart attack
4. one or both partners has gas.

The thing that goes wrong at the beginning usually goes wrong between his penis and his brain.

A good thing to remember is:
A man's excitement begins in the head, a woman's begins in the restaurant.

If there is even a hint of a problem, instead of saying, "For this I got undressed," try, "it's okay."

The only bigger lie is his: "This never happened to me before."

THE CONDOM CONVERSATION

Before you consider "doing it," you need to bring up condoms. Except for manufacturers, advertisers, and sellers, few people call condoms "swell."

"Must I wear one all the time?" a guy might ask.

Tell him, "Even in the supermarket when you're paying for your food."

"But my last girlfriend wasn't insistent at the beginning," he might argue.

His last girlfriend was a jerk.

His biggest argument might be along the lines of: "I can't feel anything with a condom."

Like he "feels" anything without it.

The simplest way to phrase it might be: "I'd like you to put on a condom after we have foreplay."

He's not for you if he asks, "What's a condom?"

Or for anyone else if he asks, "What's foreplay?"

If he's resistant and balky, bring the subject up on a later date.

With him.

Or with someone else.

WHAT IS A RELATIONSHIP?

According to women:
—a connection that leads to a starter house and children.

According to men:
—a connection that doesn't necessarily last as long as Hanukkah and leads to absolutely nothing other than regular oral sex.

•

What should you do if you suspect you are in a relationship? Or on the brink of one?

If you're a man, you needn't tell anyone until it becomes "serious." At that point you needn't bother. Everyone on Planet Earth or at least everyone within two hundred miles of where she and her mother live has heard.

•

If you're a woman, do *not* tell him. He may not even notice.

10 THINGS YOU'RE PROBABLY DOING TOGETHER

1. having sex
2. renting movies after going for dinner
3. renting movies *instead* of dinner
4. *not* making it to the final credits
5. *not* making it to the video store
6. spending a good part of the weekend together
7. horizontally
8. seeing each other during the week
9. calling him just to say "hi"
10. calling him just to say:
    a. your parakeet's been saying his name
    b. it's hard to concentrate at work
    c. his haircut is fine. You were only kidding
    d. you love *nibbling* his pointy ears.

FROM BOB TO ROB

I'm not sure what to do about Rob," said an acquaintance I'll call Liz, one evening on the phone.

"I thought it was Bob," I said.

"Bob was the guy I used to see. Rob's the one I see now. It's definitely not going anywhere."

I reminded her that it hadn't gone anywhere with Bob either. Except directly to Rob.

Liz went on. "Every time we're together he checks out. It's like he's not all there." She waited for my reaction. To see if I got her drift.

I got her drift about this "checked-out" guy. I majored in "not all theres."

"Rob sounds just like Bob," I said.

"He is."

"C'mon."

Liz thought for a few seconds, then said, "Actually, Rob was married when he was in his twenties. Bob never was. And Rob and I get together for the entire weekend through late Sunday afternoon. With Bob, it was Friday *or* Saturday."

"Any other differences?"

Liz nodded. "One's nickname begins with B. The other begins with R."

A different initial consonant. Plus Sunday afternoons. In the world of dating, that's progress.

IS HE DATING MATERIAL?

1. When a man says he is sensitive and understanding and knows how to listen to a woman, he means he'll lower the volume at half-time.

2. Men like to tell us they are in touch with their feminine side. What they mean is that they can make fettuccine Alfredo or take their town shirts to the laundry now that they don't have wives.

3. When a man talks a lot about his ex-wife before you finished your entrée, it usually means that even though he is legally divorced, she is still the main event.

4. When a man talks a lot about his mother before you've ordered dinner, she is still his *Mona Lisa* and you won't even be in the frame.

5. When a man talks on and on about everything before you've gotten to the restaurant, chances are he would be better off with:
   a. a pulpit
   b. a puppet
   c. a lobotomy
   d. his mother.

6. If you meet an accountant who spends one solid hour explaining the benefits of bonds and mutual funds, and what in life can be a tax deduction besides a date with you, then instead of saying "your work sounds fascinating" and giving him your phone number when he asks for it, you should say you are moving to France.

7. It is difficult to date after ending a long-term relationship.

8. It is harder to have a relationship.

9. It is virtually impossible to have a relationship with a picky eater.

10. If a man discusses his food allergies with you and the waiter or goes berserk when two foods on his plate touch, it is in your best interest to date others.

11. Unless the others are orators.

12. It's a toss-up which is harder to take: orators or picky eaters.

13. Long periods of celibacy are preferable to both.

14. Celibacy—thank heaven—is not a terminal disease.

15. Or interminable.

16. However, despite what they tell you in magazine articles, the new celibacy is no different from the old.

17. Even though I spend an inordinate amount of time analyzing, probing, obsessing, and ruminating, I strongly believe that we know exactly what the deal will (or will not) be within two seconds of a first meeting.

18. Much of the time we pretend we don't.

19. If a man jumps from one relationship to the next with no time to grieve, reflect, or grow, it might mean that he practices denial, has trouble with closeness, or cannot look inward.

20. If a man has not been in a relationship for a very long time and doesn't know or care why or claims it is

because he has not met the right woman, chances are that he cannot go inward, outward, or anywhere.

21. One difference between dating now and dating then is that I am less attracted to a man with a degree than I am to a man with a wok.

22. At the beginning, if a man indicates through actions and words that he wants sex and only sex, he probably wants a 20-year-old or something not too meaningful, so you should definitely move on.

23. Unless he looks like Liam Neeson.

24. When a man thinks it's great that you have a child, he sees you as:
    a. a decent, flexible, responsible person;
    b. a decent, flexible, responsible person who will no doubt help him with his kids and not want more with him;
    c. a good bet for a serious relationship;
    d. a good bet for a serious relationship, but in the meantime when he has his recurring bronchial infections, you'll help him clear his mucus with your homemade chicken soup.

25. Another difference between dating now and dating then is that I am less attracted to a man with polish than I am to a man with a soul.

26. When dating a man who says he is thrilled you love your work, he usually means:
    a. he finds you interesting;
    b. he likes independent, self-sufficient women;
    c. he likes independent, self-sufficient women because they're too busy to notice that he's unemployed, overweight, and glued to NBA games, and because they won't make financial or emotional demands.

27. Another difference between dating now and dating then is that now I don't let them win at Ping-Pong.

28. Or anything else.

29. If you sense a man doesn't get you and you don't get him or like him or find him engaging, it is not a good idea to play any games.

30. It is also not a good idea to make any decisions about a man, or where a relationship is or isn't going, the week before your period.

31. When a man tells you that you remind him of his ex-wife, check his eyes. If there are daggers, run. If there is wistfulness and sparks, there's something there he likes.

32. Chemistry is chemistry no matter how much he earns or what your family and the piano tuner think.

33. Wonderful men may leave you cold. Wonderful men may leave you. It's often not personal. Or understandable. We don't click with everyone. We're not supposed to.

34. Most dates are between "this could be it" and Dracula.

35. Most dates are between a 37" short and a 41" long.

36. When a man says he needs space, what he might mean is:
   a. he is afraid of closeness;
   b. he is afraid of being vulnerable;
   c. he is afraid of losing his power;
   d. he is afraid of losing his mind;
   e. he is very superficial and sees you're not a "10."

37. When a man says he doesn't want to get married, what he really means is: *he doesn't want to get married.*

38. Men like to say that they are not like other men. What they mean is that they are exactly like every other man who says that.

MAJOR HUMPS:
KIDS AND PARENTS

"Who just called you 'Mom'?" asked a man I'd met while giving a workshop. He taught in the room next to mine, and now we were on the phone.

"My daughter," I told him. It hadn't come up when he borrowed my chalk that I had a child or didn't.

"Your daughter," he said. Those were his next and final words. They were followed by a click.

That was that. The End of Him. We never had our date.

•

Sometimes it seems our children and parents appear—in conversation or in person—for just one reason: *to screw things up.*

1. Kids

Except for the instructor in the adjoining classroom, who may have been a child-hater, a mother-hater, or had 11 kids of his own, no man ever checked out of my life before really checking in, because I have a child.

Grant it, when she was very young, my daughter made more than one man squirm. Like when she walked around humming Dum, Dum, Dee Dum to the tune of "Here Comes the Bride" when a fellow I'd been dating was having dinner at our house. And in front of another with a hairline that receded, she asked me, "How come every man you date is bald?"

•

69

They weren't *all* bald.

Robert had hair. Robert had daughters, too, which made dealing with mine not so foreign. One evening when he and I were on the way out to the theater, she got a stomach virus. Guess who cleaned up the puke. On the nights I taught, he baby-sat for her, which involved dinner, cleaning up, and a story. Once when I was overwhelmed and overtired from single mothering and working, he held me close and said, "Some days are like that" as if he really meant it.

The family picture was not as rosy when we did things as a fivesome with his two daughters and mine. Especially when we all piled into Robert's car.

The Hump Fight would erupt.

The hump in the back was the protuberance on the floor in the middle. Sitting there meant less leg room. For the girls, it was the pits. His daughters thought mine should sit there. She had the shortest legs. Mine thought his two should alternate. They were older and more mature.

His daughters yelled at each other. Both had words with mine.

Our Brady Bunch "quality outings" became Sunday Afternoons in Hell.

When one or both have children, there's bound to be Major Humps.

And lumps.

•

"How can you stand him, Ma?" my daughter asked about an artist I once dated.

I stood him until he bought her a set of crayons and a pad. Excitedly, she opened them and began to draw, but the second she committed something to the paper, he went around the bend.

"You don't know what you are doing," he yelled from

out of nowhere, his veins popping out of his face. "That's not the *right* way to draw."

His voice was shattering. She and I both flinched. I had words with him right then and there about his lashing out at my child.

And about "the right way to draw."

●

My being a mom has been "cool" to some guys. Like the kind who say "yo" and "hey." I met a significantly younger, never-married man who was wowed when I mentioned my child. On our first date, he brought me flowers. After that he brought his phlegm. His chronic bronchitis surfaced. So did his chronic cough. Had I gone any further with this ailing guy, I'd have become a Visiting Nurse.

2. Parents

In recent years, I've had an easier time with men's parents. Partly because I am older and they've been lovely. And also because more are dead.

Alive parents of people we date can create a wedge if they:

—despise you

—hit on you

—are obnoxious.

When my friend, a third-grade teacher, met her beau's parents, the mother said, "I once considered becoming an elementary schoolteacher, too, but I decided to do something interesting with my life."

Subliminally or not so subliminally, we sometimes use our parents to sabotage the deal.

A man whom I'll call Richie Rich invited me to dinner at the country club to which his family belonged. My hair was colored blonde then. My touch-up was weeks overdo.

"Nancy's hair doesn't usually look like this," he said, introducing me to his folks.

"That's right," I told *him* and *them*. "My roots are usually darker and thicker. You can see them for yourselves in a few weeks."

The woman on Richie Rich's arm had to fit in at The Club. I withdrew my application. I didn't want the job.

THINKING ABOUT THE RELATIONSHIP

Here is what dating someone means to everyone: her, him, and to the people who care or get paid to care about them.

What she is thinking:
—At least he calls the next day.
—At least he doesn't smell.
—So what if he doesn't talk.
—So what if he can't discuss feelings.
—So he's a little out of shape. He can lose those 90 extra pounds.
—Everything's a trade-off.
—At least he doesn't stink.
—Thank God, I won't be alone New Year's Eve.
—Thank God I have someone to take to Cousin Sandra's wedding.*
—Everything's a trade-off.

* Cousin Sandra is thinking the very same thing.

What he is thinking:
—She better not drop hints about "us" when we're at her Cousin Sandra's wedding.
—I'll sit through ballet. At least afterwards, I'll get laid.
—I hope she doesn't have PMS during the World Series.
—I hope she doesn't plan to "discuss our feelings" during the World Series.
—I hope she doesn't expect to be wined and dined forever.
—Everything's a trade-off. At least she likes oral sex.

What her friends are saying:
—At least this one buys her dinner.
—At least this one has a job.
—It's none of our business. She's says he's different when they're alone.

What his friends are saying:
—Looks aren't everything.
—At least she's not after his money.
—It's not our business. He says she's nice when they're alone.

What their shrinks are thinking:
—Here we go again.
—If it works, there's always her mother.
—I give it six months. Tops.

What her parents are doing:
—Calling everyone.
—Reserving the catering hall just in case.
—Thanking God.

What his parents are doing:
—Thanking God he isn't gay.

ARE YOU COMPATIBLE?

Ponder the following questions. Alone or with him. If you aren't seeing anyone, answer these questions anyway to see how you screw up.

1. Do the two of you have the same reaction to plastic-covered furniture?

2. How do you feel about taking drugs?

3. If you answered "good" to #2, can you get your own?

4. What is your favorite
   a. sleeping position
   b. political position
   c. sexual position. (If you are better with pictures than words, draw or sketch your favorite position. If you wish, you may color it in.)

5. What do you do if one person has several favorite sexual positions and the other must face Tiffany's?

6. What is the best way to handle the other's tardiness?

7. What about coming too soon?

8. How would you like your partner to be treating you a year from now?

9. If you aren't sure how to answer that, elaborate on your favorite sexual position. Again, feel free to draw.

Answer key: If you spent more than 10 minutes on this, you are analyzing and intellectualizing the relationship, rather than having it.

SEEING EACH OTHER: A QUIZ

Match the definition to the word:
    premature ejaculation
    lumps
    humps
    ex-spouses

1. What relationships and Quasimodo have in common.
2. They say less than Calvin Coolidge did.
3. Like taxes and herpes, they don't go away.
4. It's a little like stage fright.

Answers:
1. humps
2. lumps
3. ex-spouses
4. premature ejaculation

PART THREE

SEX

SEXUAL SNAGS AND SURPRISES

The following fears and joys are integral to sex:

Women's Fears—What if:
—he's not turned on by my body?
—it turns him on more than my mind?
—he's just using me?
—he doesn't use me well?
—he's a total dud?
—I hear angels singing while he hears his mother *kvetch?*
—we both hear those very same angels. How long can the music last?

Men's Fears—What if:
—I can't satisfy her?
—I can't perform as well as other men she's been with? More likely: What if I can't perform?

Women's Joys:
—shopping
—cuddling
—closeness
—coming
—coming, coming, and coming.

Men's Joys:
—performing well
—oral anything
—satisfying my partner
—satisfying my partner before noon on Sunday so I can watch the entire game.

SEX AGAIN

Everything comes up with sex. If we're lucky. It's where our
basic truths come out. And where there are packs of lies.
Certain aspects of sex have changed. Others never will.

	Men	*Women*
Why did we have sex in the past?	For pleasure.	For procreation and jewelry.
Why do we have sex now?	For pleasure.	For procreation, pleasure, and bonding. For longer and greater pleasure.
What does the sex act include?	Intercourse	Kissing necking petting unhooking bras flinging clothes around the room touching exploring heavy breathing more kissing more touching her first orgasm intercourse his orgasm his concern for her satisfaction her satisfaction cuddling giggling conversation a snack

Men	Women
	more cuddling a back rub sleep breakfast a parting kiss in the morning a phone call later to chat. (Jewish women: All of the above plus dinner.)
What is foreplay? Foreplay?	The first 10 activities in the above "sex act" list.
Describe your best time? Just under three minutes.	A weekend with a sexy man. A weekend with a sexy man where there's a roaring fire in the fireplace and a Jacuzzi. A weekend with all of the above plus a vibrator.
What is something a sexual partner has said to you while making love that was more than a wee bit alienating?	For this, you woke me? Peach, I think we should paint the room peach.	I was calling out, "I'm close, I'm close," and he said, "Close to what?"

SEXUAL RULES
TO REMEMBER

1. The only time a man does not want sex is right after sex.
2. The sex act is the sex act according to a man.
3. To a woman, it's sometimes a scene.
4. Most men prefer the missionary position.
5. Women prefer to face Bloomingdale's.

A LITTLE SURPRISE

My cultivated friend, Elaine, went out with a teacher whom I'll call Victor. Or, as she called him, Vic.

Their first several dates were pleasant enough. Vic was well-versed in many subjects, including the Brontës, his mom, and his tenure. Everything was dandy until they got undressed. There, on his jockey shorts, embroidered in navy letters, right across the pee-pee was the phrase, "I'd go to great lengths for you," and beside it, a picture of (Oh God!) a twelve-inch ruler.

Elaine sat on the bed staring at the little message. She wondered if Vic wore these wordy shorts because he thought they'd turn her on. She wondered if he got them at some tacky souvenir shop or if some demented girlfriend once bought them for him as a joke. Mostly she wondered if he had gotten them just for this occasion or if he had always been a nerd.

"I wanted to laugh. I wanted to scream. I wanted to run away," she told me.

There was no way she was going to have sex with Victor or Vic. So she looked him straight in the eye and said, "Listen Vic, I love the printed word. I really do, but I firmly believe it belongs on paper. Seeing that sentence on your penis is giving me the creeps."

That was that. They got dressed in silence. No reason for any more great lengths.

TURNING THE TABLES

A friend of mine pretty much wrote off a guy she'd started seeing when they had the Condom Conversation. He said he wouldn't wear one. That was that. It was clear to her now, why at 46 he'd never had a wife, a live-in, a longtime relationship, or a pet.

Still, it was two A.M. at the end of their fifth date and despite his murky warning signals, there was something about him she liked, more about waking up alone on Sunday she hated, and a half-empty bed for too long.

"You can stay over, but no fooling around," she said.

Guess what? He agreed.

They got into bed—she in a print silk nightshirt and he in his underwear—and after a close-mouthed little kiss went to sleep.

In the morning, he rolled on top of her.

She surprised herself when she responded naturally and didn't push him away. Still in her bedclothes, she moved easily with him, letting nature take its course.

The rub of this rub? To her amazement, she came. Just

like that. Fully nightshirted. With nothing oral, manual, or penile.

For her, a definite first.

"What about me?" asked Mr. Never-Been-Married-Or-Seriously-Involved-and-Wouldn't-Wear-a-Condom.

Him?

She used her hand on his you-know-what in a way that would have pleased Dr. Ruth.

But he kept going into neutral.

Up and down. Up and down went her hand until it could go no more.

"This is like sawing," she said. "Let's eat breakfast instead."

They did. Then afterwards, he said, "I wouldn't mind trying again."

But she'd had hers. And was tired and relaxed. So in the words of Every Man she said, "I already came."

They read sections of the newspaper and he suggested having sex again. He even agreed to a condom. But her TV was on. The Giants had scored. And in the words of almost Every Man she'd ever known said, "I don't want to miss the game."

She wasn't a fan, but she watched anyway with Mr. Didn't-Finish at her side. The Giants won. My friend was jubilant. Victory was her cry.

THINGS WE DO FOR LUST

Sometimes it's pure lust. And sometimes it's less or more. Here are nine friends' very best lust stories:

My friend, Betsy, said it would never happen today. But it was the casual, pre-AIDS seventies when men weren't required to wear condoms and she was still wearing fur. She had recently split up with her husband and the only thing keeping her warm was the black diamond mink coat her mother had bought her as a condolence present.

She was riding up the elevator of her building one evening after work with a very appealing man whom she had been flirting with in the laundry room, the lobby, at their mailboxes, and whenever they were standing at the bus stop together on the way to work. She had let him know that her husband was out of the picture. He had told her she looked smashing in her mink.

And he told her again in the elevator.

"After you drop your things off, why don't you come up for a drink?" she said as the door opened at his floor.

He had a better idea. He'd take her out for dinner. But only if she wore her mink.

She did. Twenty minutes later she rang his bell. In her mink. With nothing underneath. They never made it to a restaurant. Or got together again.

With and without fur coats, we have all done things for lust. Little things and big things. Things we did when we were younger and more impulsive. And things that make us squirm.

Alice, a real estate agent, still squirms about a "matching shower curtain" she once made. A man she absolutely flipped over had just redone his bathroom with wall tiles that had a geometric design. Alice took a few tiles home, figured out the proportions and pattern of the circles, squares, and triangles, and appliquéd them onto a shower curtain in the exact same colors and size. The result of her weeks of labor astounded everyone: her, him, and his new girlfriend, who began showering regularly in his redecorated bathroom soon after the new appliqué curtain was hung.

Years ago, my friend Bob, a Wall Street stockbroker, answered a personal ad in *New York Magazine* in which the woman described herself as a "beautiful, bright, blonde nonsmoker who enjoys laughter." She did not say, however, that she was laughing and not smoking in Fort Lauderdale.

Until she responded to his letter. By phone.

Bob felt "that tingle" the second she said hello. Her voice was so sexy and inviting and their conversation was so charged that within an hour they were deciding between Paris and Hawaii for their honeymoon and naming their first child and their dog. She suggested that even though they could "feel" their connection and were absolutely sure that this could very well be "it," they should, because they were so far apart, think things over carefully and sleep on all they'd said.

Except Bob was too excited to sleep. The next morning he talked about her to everyone in his office. At lunchtime he made a plane reservation to Fort Lauderdale for that Friday, then called to let her know that he was on his way.

Bob spent two days in Florida with his "bright, beautiful blonde." He never spoke about what they did that weekend. But they never did it again.

To spy on her sometime lover, Jane, a 36-year-old attorney, used to plop herself twice a day for more weeks than she is willing to admit across the street from his apartment, where she had a full view of both the building entrance and his living room and where no one would ever dream of finding her: in a Christian Science Reading Room.

A decade ago, Suzanne, now 29, had a summer romance with a fellow she met at the beach. Since they were both living with their parents at their family cottages, the only way they could be alone was to go off into the woods. Suzanne got the worst case of poison ivy in the worst place on her body. Fortunately, her mother and the dermatologist who treated her didn't probe or judge.

Heidi, a fashion designer, wasn't the only person squirming when she joined an a cappella singing group to be near a man she desired. Heidi can't sing a note on key. A cappella or any way. The man, like the other long-standing members of the group, sang beautifully. Heidi became appealing to him *after* she closed her mouth.

There have been times when, for the sake of lust, we've concocted little white lies. Linda, a physician, once had a lover who did not feel very comfortable hanging out in her apartment. To put him at ease, she'd spend hours preparing wonderful gourmet dishes and then tell him they were leftovers.

"I've got a little chicken, rice pilaf, and spinach casserole in the frig from yesterday," she'd call and casually say. "I'll just reheat them."

She swears that the man never caught on. Or had an inkling the food was not "just reheated." Even when she served him an entire roasted chicken.

Those little lies we tell for lust may lead to something enduring. Something, as they say, with legs. That was the case with my friend Arlene.

Arlene, a phone systems sales rep, closed a deal with Roy, a businessman, whom she found utterly irresistible. A week after the system was installed, she called to make sure it was working properly, then asked him for referrals. A week later she invited him to lunch as a way of thanking him for the leads. She subtly let him know she was available and interested. He not-so-subtly let her know that his company never needed a new phone system. They got married three months later and are still together today.

Speaking of legs, my friend Nick once made a serious attempt to use *his* for the sake of lust. Nick became obsessed with a dancer he'd often see while jogging in Central Park. He found out she had a boyfriend, but things between them were strained, and that she taught ballet at Finis Jhung Studios on Broadway.

He bought a pair of ballet slippers and enrolled in her Basic Beginners 1.

As an all-round jock and onetime member of his college crew and basketball teams, Nick assumed ballet would come easily. As he ran across the mirrored room and did exercises at the bars, nothing came at all. He was the only man among fifteen women. Humiliated. And a klutz.

Still, he wanted to impress the teacher, who looked even better in her leotard, but as the weeks went by and the class pliéd, Nick definitely looked worse.

He didn't give up. At the end of the 10-week session, he asked about her Basic Beginners 2 class. She told him politely that he wasn't ready. More obsessed and "in lust" than before, he enrolled again in Basic Beginners 1.

Nick's ballet showed no improvement. The teacher's relationship with her boyfriend apparently did. They moved to Europe together where she joined a notable dance company.

A picture of her performing is hanging on Nick's wall. Right next to his ballet slippers.

A SEX QUIZ

Use the following words to answer 1 through 5:
pu-lease
fix the siding on the house
talk
talk
talk

1. What men want to do after sex.
2. What women want to do after sex.
3. What women want to do before sex.
4. What women want to do instead of sex.
5. What men want to do instead of sex.

Answers:
1. fix the siding on the house
2. talk
3. talk
4. talk
5. pu-lease

Key: If you missed more than one, you are clueless about "the other."

87 THINGS THAT ARE BETTER THAN SEX

In *Scent of a Woman*, Al Pacino's character, Frank Slade, says there is nothing—absolutely *nothing*—that is anywhere near as wonderful as sex. But, he immediately adds, driving a Ferrari is definitely a distant second. As we left the movie theater, my friends and I wondered if we could think of 10 things that are better than sex.

"Ten?" my friend Harvey gasped. "I can't even come up with one."

His girlfriend, Linda, had a different response. She asked, "Only 10?"

No. Not just 10. When we all got rolling, we came up with a whole bunch just in the area of shopping. The following are 87 things that we feel are better than sex:

1. Spending two hours in the back room at Loehmann's.

2. Having a friend who is a fashion designer and being her sample shoe size.

3. Actually *liking* the image you see of yourself in the dressing room mirror while trying on bathing suits.

4. *Not* having to diet.

5. Watching Baryshnikov dance.

6. Watching Baryshnikov sit.

7. Skiing in fresh packed powder.

8. Hitting every mogul right.

9. Taking a hike on a quiet, beautiful trail with the sun shining.

10. Sitting outdoors in the winter with the sun on your face in a spot where you're protected from the wind.

11. Having a good laugh.

12. Having your child get your joke.

13. Having *anyone* get your joke.

14. Chocolate cake.

15. Chocolate mousse cake.

16. Being mistaken for Michelle Pfeiffer.

17. Driving a convertible along a country road on a warm, summer day with the top down.

18. Driving on the highway with songs from the 1960s blasting on the radio.

19. In Scrabble, getting the *q* and the *u*.

20. Getting a triple-word score using all seven letters.

21. Coming up with a clever retort while you're still at the party rather than in the car going home.

22. Being in the company of very smart, witty people and having a wonderfully stimulating conversation.

23. Being the only one in a roomful of smart people to know the final answer on "Jeopardy!"

24. Having your stretch marks disappear after childbirth.

25. Returning to your normal jean size after childbirth.

26. Sharing your innermost, scariest feelings with a very good friend and finding out she has had them too.

27. Watching the tomatoes you planted come up.

28. Seeing your tulips bloom.

29. Not recognizing the captain of your high school football team, who recognizes you immediately because, he says, you haven't changed a bit.

30. Knowing that in certain ways, which he couldn't possibly get and you are not about to explain, you *have* changed.

31. Buying designer clothes below cost.

32. Telling a know-it-all relative she overpaid for her designer clothes.

33. Playing the piano.

34. Playing the Mozart sonata you couldn't play back then.

35. Playing the piano when you feel like it and not when your mother tells you to.

36. Not taking lessons.

37. Not playing for the relatives.

38. Making music with other people.

39. Making music with other people on key.

40. Going to your twentieth high school reunion and having the fellow you secretly loved way back then ask you to dance the first slow one.

41. Having the pool at your parents' Florida condominium all to yourself.

42. Not being dragged away from the pool in the middle of the afternoon to get to an early-bird dinner.

43. Cuddling with your cat or dog, who makes you feel that you are absolutely "it."

44. Cuddling with a mate who feels that same way.

45. Sitting in a Jacuzzi in the Rockies after a day of skiing.

46. Finding the perfect blouse for the skirt that has been in the back of the closet for three years because nothing ever looked right with it.

47. Getting the skirt over your hips.

48. Watching *Casablanca, The African Queen,* and *Auntie Mame* again and again and again.

49. Listening to Sinatra sing "One for My Baby."

50. Listening to Van Cliburn play Tchaikovsky's Piano Concerto No. 1.

51. Having your child fall asleep in your arms.

52. Finding a $50 bill under the sofa cushion in a hotel lobby that no one comes to claim.

53. Inheriting money from a relative you didn't know existed.

54. Getting under a goose-down comforter on a cold winter night.

55. Reading an engrossing novel, which takes you to another realm.

56. Having your two-year-old child nap.

57. Having a quick but badly needed afternoon nap and waking up totally refreshed.

58. Having parents who baby-sit.

59. Saying "I love you" to someone.

60. Waking up before you have to and going back to sleep.

61. Having your haircut turn out *exactly* like the one in the magazine you showed to your hairdresser.

62. After being bumped from a flight, getting out on the next one and flying first-class.

63. Watching reruns of "The Mary Tyler Moore Show."

64. Finding a pair of chic-looking shoes you can walk in.

65. Getting a massage from someone who *really* knows how to give one.

66. Drinking freshly squeezed orange juice in the morning.

67. Dancing with a great partner.

68. Walking along the beach in the morning and at dusk.

69. Having a hand to hold.

70. Standing at the bottom of the Grand Canyon and looking up.

71. Reading on the sofa next to someone you love.

72. Watching the snow fall with someone you love.

73. Being inside on a cold winter day and watching the logs burn in your fireplace.

74. Getting your car going after a snowstorm.

75. Getting your first story published.

76. Finding your old 45s in your mother's attic and a turntable on which you can play them.

77. Being able to set up the ball in volleyball.

78. Being able to cross the wake waterskiing.

79. Getting up on one ski.

80. Staying up on one ski for the entire ride.

81. Staying up.

82. Knowing that even in some small way, you have made a difference.

83. Knowing yourself.

84. Having a friend with whom you can discuss and giggle about sex.

85. Fantasizing about sex.

86. Writing about sex.

87. And last—but far from least—remembering sex.

FROM LOOSE ENDS TO HARD KNOTS

DATING PATTERNS

Dating patterns, while not as decorative as china or wall-paper patterns, have their own unique designs. Several factors contribute to the type of involvement. They include:
—chemistry
—geography
—no other academic subjects
—flexibility
—compatibility
—adaptability
—tolerance level
—testosterone level
—sea level
—the depth of each's feelings
—the depth of each's despair
—timing
—timing, timing, and timing.

FROM LOOSE ENDS TO HARD KNOTS

1. *Very casual*
There is no agenda, rules, or long-term plans. It's more like:
—when we both dig it,
—when you or the circus come to town.

This works for people who live in different time zones. Or when at least one of the two is heavily into:
—work
—children
—debt
—drugs
—other pursuits
—other people.
The good news about "very casual" is you can still look. The bad news is you're still looking.

2. Casual

The person is "sort of" in the picture or at the very least in the frame when:
—you want an escort to a family wedding so you won't be the eleventh one at the table again and without a dance partner when the band plays "All the Way."
—you want sex without strings
—you want strings, but not with him
—the other person you are seeing is seeing another person
—the other person you are seeing is acting like a little shit
—there is no other person in your life. This is what's available.

3. Not Exactly Monogamous:

This is similar to casual but less occasional and random. It usually includes: at least one weekend night, some holidays, advance planning, and *lies*.
For example:
If he says, "Susan and Jim want to double with us. How's Thursday?"
Her answers might be:
1. I have to check when my aunt is coming,
   or
2. That may be the evening I'm taking a class.
   She means: She's waiting for her main man to call.

The major drawback here is: At the height of passion she might scream, "Oh Harry, Harry, Harry," when she means "Oh Phil, Oh Phil, Oh Phil."

4. *Monogamous:*

This means you're seeing him, he's seeing you, and neither is doing anything intimate with anyone else except discussing this relationship with your friends. It may lead to:
—new heights
—greater awareness
—total bliss
—the altar
—termination
—heartbreak
—therapy
—or to Numbers 1, 2, and 3.

It may also lead to:
—counting on someone
—knowing yourself
—at least for the time being, everlasting love.

THREE Rs:
REJECTS, RETREADS,
AND RECYCLES

Rejecting, recycling, and retreading are often part of The Deal. What do these three Rs mean?

reject: a person, who anywhere from the onset to years down the pike, has been told to take a flying leap.

101

Why a man is rejected:

1. He didn't turn her on.
2. She found someone who did.
3. He didn't satisfy her.
4. She found someone who's trying.
5. She wanted to get married. He wanted to get laid.
6. She didn't want to be rejected first.
7. Whatever reasons she gave him, The Truth is probably #5.

Why a woman is rejected:

1. She was not a deaf-mute.
2. Or a 10.
3. He found a 10.
4. He found happiness at his computer.
5. She wanted to get married. He wanted to get laid.
6. She is dying for a baby. He's already fathered three.
7. Whatever reason he gave her, The Truth includes #1 and #5.

Verbal rejection

The following are tried-and-true lines:
- —It's not you. It's me.
- —I need time.
- —I need space.
- —I need an enema.
- —An old beau reappeared. We're trying to work it out.
- —My therapist says I'm not ready.
- —I can't make a commitment until my prison term is up.
- —I hope we can still be friends. (Ouch!)

Nonverbal rejection

- —Keeping one's testosterone to oneself
- —Disappearing without a word
- —Disappearing in bed
- —A knee in the groin
- —A can of mace

The Rejected Person's Response:
Hers: You and that slut deserve each other.
His: What does he have that I don't have besides a raging boner?

●

retread: a person with whom you try again for one or more of these reasons:
1. he's available again
2. he's *still* available
3. and better than nothing
4. at least the sex was good
5. at least the sex wasn't awful
6. you realize that in the whole scheme of things he isn't such a creep
7. you're tired of the whole scheme.

●

Successful Retreading

My friend, Annie, age 37, sat next to a man at a business luncheon and called me that afternoon with a bulletin.

"He's *The One*" she said in a voice I'd never heard before in the decade I had known her. They'd met in the late eighties, but he hadn't thrilled her then. Neither had any other man in many, many years.

Within a month they were seeing each other four to six times a week. Then Annie moved into his apartment. They got married within a year.

"It sure happened fast with you," I said.

Only it wasn't fast at all. Thirty-seven years.

"It's the right guy at the right time," she said.

And emotionally the right place.

Verbal retreading: calling an erstwhile beau with the pretense you are enlisting him for the very thing he majored in.

Examples:
a. the computer maven to help you format discs
b. the lusty guy from the wrong side of the tracks with whom the sex was heavenly (forget pretense here)
c. the shrink because it's Christmas and you need a shoulder and ear.

Holiday Retreading

You can't face Christmas and New Year's alone. You're feeling great despair. You call an erstwhile beau, a psychotherapist, who majored in "Holiday Blues."

He is thrilled to hear your voice again. He can speak to you at greater length between "psychological hours" or when "their time" is up.

He makes a house call to your apartment that evening. He listens and nods quite well. One nod leads to another. All nods lead to your bed.

It doesn't exactly happen. It's *exactly* like before.

"I don't understand," he says, throwing up his arms. "It's never like this when I'm with other women."

You don't understand either, but *here*—where he is not The Detached Listener—he doesn't give a rusty how you feel, which is lonelier than if you'd been alone.

You spend two more evenings together, including New Year's Eve. Then as your baggage and his baggage become too heavy to lift, you part.

Your holiday despair has lifted. Your normal depression has returned. And he is back in his office saying little more than "uh huh."

•

recycle: your friend's ex-beau or spouse with whom you give it a try for one of more of these reasons:
1. The two of you had a lot in common.
2. The two of you had chemistry.
3. The two of you have neither of the above. He's the only one who calls.

4. You want to see if those things she bragged about are really true or if she was trying to make you jealous.

5. You want to prove you have "the stuff" to keep him even if she did not.

6. You're not trying to prove a blessed thing. It's been a while.

●

Elder Recycling: The Chicken Soup Brigade

When a 72-year-old friend's wife died, he was, for the first time in his entire life, suddenly alone.

For about three minutes.

From seven states, women who had been her friends, their friends, or his friends in the second grade arrived with their best dishes, soups, and stews.

Within a year, the widower remarried. Ten months later he got divorced. The Chicken Soup Brigade is back again and lined up at his door.

●

After my Uncle George died, my Aunt Lucy, his widow, was nourished by the Chicken Soup Brigade. For one week.

Then she was on her own.

Her first foray into the social world was a seven-day Caribbean cruise. Shortly after boarding, she met a lovely, congenial widower. He mentioned his wife had died just two months before so Aunt Lucy decided not to push it. After the cruise, she'd invite him to the theater. In the meantime, she'd chat in passing.

Except there was no passing. Or anything resembling a "meantime."

The first night, the lovely widower appeared at dinner with a woman on his arm. She was at his side for every activity, including shuffleboard, and at every port. The last night at the captain's dinner came the announcement: *They were engaged.*

Home or away, on land or at sea, first prize is: a man with a pulse.

•

Fortunately, Aunt Lucy has a life. She travels, plays cards, and has friends. A couple in her circle invited her for bridge. Her partner was an arthritic widower who insisted on trumping her ace.

Despite Aunt Lucy's preference for smarter, weller men, she and the fourth began dating. When he started pushing for a commitment, Aunt Lucy called it quits.

"Any regrets?" I asked her.

"Not really," she said. Admittedly she gets lonely and misses Uncle George.

"It's hard being on your own when you've had The Real Thing," she said.

It's no great shakes when you haven't.

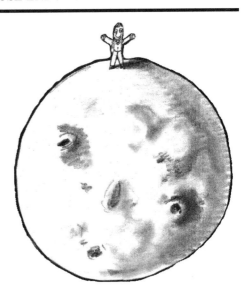

WHAT IS SPACE?

space (spās) n.
(*according to* Webster's)
—the unlimited or indefinitely great three-dimensional expanse in which all material objects are located and all events occur.
—an interval of time; a while.

(*according to most men*)
"I need space" means: I need intervals and a while in another:
—apartment
—city
—planet
—woman.

DIFFERENT TYPES OF RELATIONSHIPS

The following range from little wedges to big time:

	One's	*The Other's*
perfect vacation	visiting every church	rolling over
personality	a ball of fire	networking with snails
philosophy of relating	let it all hang out	"No Trespassing"
libido	in overdrive	at the lost and found

●

Different ages:

If she's in her twenties or thirties and he's much older, it helps if she likes to shop. Or decorate. Or nap.

If, however, he's much younger, it could mean very good sex. As my friend, Lisa, who only sees guys at least six years younger, puts it, "If I'm going to take off all my clothes, there'd better be a reason."

For a twentysomething woman, the younger man may only work on paper. Sex might be great, but he's got no time between driver's ed and the SATs.

Older women and young men have no shared past. That can make relating harder.

"Where were you the day Kennedy was assassinated?" I asked an aspiring artist on our first date at the cheapest restaurant in Manhattan.

In 1963, he wasn't.

●

Different places:

It's possible to have a relationship between Pittsburgh and Detroit. Both people must be motivated. And more than a little detached.

Erma lives with her young children in Boston where she's a tenured biology professor. Hal has a government job in Washington, D.C. They met on vacation and were equally smitten. Yet equally committed to stay put.

They spend weekends and holidays together. And lots of time on planes. It works. They're happy. They want the same things: to be together as much as they can. And to be apart even more.

●

Different classes:

I'm not talking here about a fourth grader with a fifth, but about two people who socially or intellectually are in totally different ballparks, like:

—an art historian and a bus driver

—a status-seeking member of the nouveau riche and someone who can't spell Saks

—Lady and the Tramp

—a Brooklyn Jew and a Sutton Place WASP

—a WASP with anyone who isn't.

●

I once dated a plumber. Not a plumber who was really a writer and writing The Novel on weekends. He was *really* a plumber.

Initially we were both intrigued. The men I'd known did "paperwork." The women he'd known "did malls."

Our differences seeped in though. It started during Charades. He held up two fingers and made the sign for book. I called out, "Moby-Dick."

"Ma, you don't know," my daughter whispered.

"I do," I told her. "He only knows one book."

It <u>was</u> *Moby-Dick*.

I didn't care that the printed word turned him on less than a stuffed-up toilet, but he was "nowhere" and more than a little depressed when he wasn't using his plunger.

●

I know a woman—an MD in her late fifties—who got married for the second time. When I met her thirteen years ago, her first husband had just left, her grown children were gone, and she was in her first year of med school. Her friends had pooled their resources and were paying her tuition.

A cool woman, I then thought. Such courage! Such ambition! Such devoted friends!

I bumped into her last year at the supermarket and she told me she had a new husband.

"Is he a doctor?" I asked.

"He's a hairdresser."

I was more than a little surprised. "Where'd you meet a hairdresser?" I asked. Obviously not at the beauty parlor. She looked like she hadn't been.

"We knew each other years ago," she said, smiling. "He's really great."

Goose bumps appeared on my arms. "Is it different from the first marriage?"

"Oh God, yes! This guy gets me. This one's great." Her smile widened. "I'm a really lucky lady."

Yes. And cooler than I'd thought.

FOUR GREAT REASONS TO SPLIT

1. *He's ambivalent*

His body may be in the same room as yours, but his spirit—if he has one—is closer to the moon. The quickest way to spot ambivalence is to have a healthy dose of your own. If you don't (or think you don't), pay attention to these things:

—he doesn't hold your gaze
—he doesn't hold your hand
—he calls you Mary. Your name is Ann.
—he doesn't call when he says he will
—he calls, but doesn't show up on time
—he may show up with a song in his heart, but anger is lurking beneath
—no matter what he says or does, The Truth will show up in bed.

2. *He's addicted*

It's in the eyes, the lies, and the mood swings. Substance abusers can be tough to spot, though. You sometimes have to find the substance.

●

My friend, Josie, was dating a businessman who six months after oral surgery was still taking massive doses of Percodan. She didn't make too much of it. She comes from a family that wouldn't leave for vacation until they finished all the milk in the frig. She assumed he had the same Let's-Use-Everything-Up mentality.

But when he went to the men's room three times during *The Fugitive*, she suspected it wasn't to pee.

"Something wrong with your bladder?" she asked when it was over.

He shook his head.

"What did you think about the movie?" she said.

"I liked it," he said.

"As much as the white stuff under your nose?"

"What white stuff?"

"The coke," she said, in a voice so loud that everyone in Cinemas 1 through 6 could hear.

He was history before the credits finished rolling.

•

I thought Henry, a man I was getting to know, was cranky at the beach because he didn't like the sun. I thought he was moody on Sunday evenings because he had to part with his kids.

I thought, I thought, I thought, I thought.

I kept coming up with reasons why Henry was shutting me out. He was sexy, street smart, and funny. There was poetry in his soul.

"I see us as two trees growing together through the forest of life," he told me one night.

How romantic! How touching! It was only later when I found a vial of white powder on the bathroom sink that I realized his drugs were kicking in.

"How could you put coke next to my daughter's dinosaur soap?" I could hear myself getting hysterical. With or without drugs, men certainly have that way.

"That's not just coke," he told me. "That's coke mixed with heroin." He was smiling now. A sweet smile, too. Damn it!

I swallowed hard. "Forgive me for being so stupid," I said, as calmly as I might have if he'd told me he took honey in his tea. Why give him the satisfaction of being shocked or pained?

"So what should we do?" he asked.

"We?" I said. "You're taken care of. I'm the one who could use a hobby." I wanted him to tell me that *I* was more important than drugs and he'd stop taking them for me. But that wasn't what happened.

"He would have been my man if it weren't for his drug habit," I remember telling a friend.

"And your grandmother would have been a tricycle," my friend said, "if only she had wheels."

3. He's not really single

If he has a wife, it helps to have this little piece of information before hopping into the sack.

My friend Sandra was dating a member of the "Old-Boys" Network. A Size 41-regular with a pedigree.

The condom conversation was behind them. Pleasure was ahead. He'd undressed her. Then she undressed him starting with all three pieces of his navy custom-made suit.

He got it up. Then lost it. Again and again and again. "Is it me?" she asked, feeling a wee bit baffled after using patience, "it's okays," and her hand.

He shook his head.

"I'm feeling uncomfortable," she said, still putting the onus on herself as women invariably do. "Could you share what *you* think is going on?"

"I'm married," he told her. "I thought I could do this, but I can't. Our twentieth anniversary is tomorrow and I haven't bought my wife a present."

Sandra leaped out of bed. "Were you going to tell me if you hadn't gotten limp?"

"Eventually," he said. "I want you to know something about me."

Sandra, getting dressed in layers yet, was throwing him his clothes. "I already do."

"I want you to know that this isn't really what I'm like," he said, zipping his custom-made pants.

Right.

4. *He's not really straight*

Some men don't know or admit it.* They lie, pretend, or masquerade as straight.** So how can you tell if it's him and not you? What are the signs that he's gay?

—he calls you Ralph. Your name is Joan.
—he's seen *Sunset Boulevard* more than once
—he says no one cooks like his mom
—or dresses like his mom
—the first time he plans to spend the night, he arrives with a little bottle of mouthwash
—he's over 40 and has never lived with a woman except for you-know-who
—his apartment looks like the roped-off rooms at the Palace of Versailles.
—he can't tolerate clutter, dust, and anything unfolded
—or very much about you.

* except in my neighborhood in lower Manhattan where they flaunt it.

** except in my neighborhood where they cross-dress.

THE DICK STORY

It was a Thursday—an ordinary Thursday—when I got the following call:

"Is this Nancy?" said a woman at the other end.

"Yes," I said, waiting for her to identify herself.

"It's Dick's wife."

"Whose?"

"Dick's."

"I don't know any Dicks."

Right. Like any female over 11 could utter such a thing. "Could you tell me what's going on here?" I asked.

"Monday. The fund-raiser at the Waldorf. You were there, weren't you?"

"Yes, but who are you?" I asked. "Where'd you get my number?"

"From Dick's jacket pocket. You gave it to him Monday night."

"I didn't give any Dick my number."

She went on. "You did the jitterbug, didn't you? With a guy who could really lead?"

"I danced, but my partner was a widower and his name wasn't Dick."

There was a pause. A long pause. Then she asked, "Was it Lou?"

Chills went through my entire body. "Yes," I said. "Lou. He told me he was a widower, though. I guess that means you're not dead."

"I'm not dead," she said, emphatically. "And he's not Lou." There was a long silence, then she added, "Smooth dancer, huh?"

"In my entire life, I never looked so good jitterbugging. I actually felt graceful."

She chuckled. "That's what he does."

"This isn't the first time then."

"No hon."

"I'm sorry."

"Hey," she said, with that little chuckle again. "Every so often he gets a taker, but he makes sure to leave their numbers in the same jacket pockets the day I take them to the cleaners. Has he called you yet?"

"Tuesday."

"And?"

"He wanted to come over."

"Did he?"

"No," I gulped. "Something put me off then. He called me from a pay phone."

"That's Dick."

"I never would have given him my number if I thought he had a wife."

"Well, sounds like you pretty much know what's out there."

A knot formed in my stomach. I guess I pretty much do.

She went on. "If you ever see him, you'll be very sorry." Her voice was quieter now. There was no trace of laughter anymore.

"I never would." This poor woman. This poor wife. "I'm sorry for you," I told her.

"Yeah well, I'm not sure where you've been, but that's how it is out there."

Yes.

That's how it is for some.

EPILOGUE

That pretty much covers what I have to say about dating.

I'd like to end with something uplifting and pithy, like: the more we do it, the better we get, but I'm not sure that's true. We get older. Sometimes wiser. Certainly mellower. But the fears and feelings and nausea and thrills between the sexes never really change.

In sixth or seventh grade, we attend that first school dance. The girls are huddled on one side of the gym. The boys are on the other.

There's that huge space in between.

That evening and for the rest of our lives, we're supposed to come together in the least klutzy ways we can.

Our cool peers do it easily. Or have the confidence to pretend.

Nothing changes from junior high. There are different players. Different verses. The melody's the same.

My widowed Aunt Lucy, now in her seventies, has returned to the side of the room. Whenever we talk, and we do more nowadays, we get right down to *them*.

"I've had it!" she declared during a conversation after she'd broken up with an idiot.

I reminded her that if she compares all men to her late husband, a brain and a sweet, gentle man, they'll *all* get As on the moron test.

She agreed. "A lot of men are jerks, though."

Right. The flotsam and the jetsam. The ones who are still out there. At her age. And at mine.

Sometimes when I'm on a date with a man who is going to be history within a few hours, my brain and my heart send a message down my arm, propelling my hand to start moving. It's holding a bunch of imaginary darts which I throw at an imaginary target. I make sure my date doesn't see my hand, because I like to keep on throwing.

Dating is like *that* game at the amusement park where you throw darts at the balloons. If you throw dart after dart, game after game, eventually you pop one.

For now, I wish to close with four things—the only four things—I can say with conviction after all my years of dating:
—it doesn't get easier
—your gut is your truth
—it won't work if you "fake it"
—I still require dinner.